# Martinis & Marshmallows:

## A FIELD GUIDE TO
## LUXURY TENT CAMPING

## Cara L. Schulz

### Zack Willow Publishing

Burnsville, Minnesota

Zack Willow Publishing
Cara Schulz
schulzcaral@gmail.com

Although the author and publisher have made every effort to ensure that the information in this book was correct at press time, the author and publisher do not assume and hereby disclaim any liability to any party for any loss, damage, or disruption caused by errors or omissions, whether such errors or omissions result from negligence, accident, or any other cause.

By publishing photos of, or writing about, specific products or companies, this book does not claim an affiliation with or an endorsement by those products or companies.

Martinis & Marshmallows / Cara Schulz. —1st ed.
ISBN 978-0-9912931-2-4

## Also by Cara Schulz

*(Almost) Foolproof Mead Making*

## Forthcoming Titles

*(Almost) Foolproof Hard Cider Brewing*

*Martinis & Marshmallows: Glamping Kitchens*

*This book is dedicated to my husband, Tracy, for helping make my dream a reality; my son, Justin, who is a better person than I; my parents, Lonny and Selene, who knew from the start I wasn't going to conform and love me anyway.*

# Contents

# Introduction

*"I hate camping."*

When I hear those words, I know I'm usually talking to someone whose opinion of camping has been influenced by an inappropriately aggressive fan of roughing it. There's nothing wrong with primitive camping unless you try to force everyone else to camp that way because it's the only "real" way to camp.

There are many ways to camp, and all of them are real. In this book I'll show you how an average person with a low to moderate budget can have a comfortable, relaxing, and fun camping experience.

Each chapter of this book opens with an example campsite. It's set up for a single person, a couple, or a group or family. It's also modeling a specific look. Don't feel constrained to stay within these examples; choose ideas that appeal to you, and mix and match. If you like the kitchen in one chapter, the look in another, and the tent in a third, go with that combination.

There are also products I've highlighted throughout the book. All of these are items I have bought myself, use, and recommend because I've found them to be excellent products.

My hope is that those of you who haven't camped before, or haven't enjoyed roughing-it-style camping in the past, are inspired by the ideas and photos to find you were born to camp.

# Fleeting Fantasy

# FLEETING FANTASY

Mortan a picnic but less than camping, a trysting tent is the height of romance. Part of what makes it so special is its ephemeral nature. Like Cinderella's dress, it's not meant to last. When balancing aesthetics, comfort, and functionality, focus on aesthetics first, then comfort, with just enough functionality to get by for a few hours. Privacy, though, is a must. Getting arrested for indecent exposure would be memorable, but it's not a good way to spend an anniversary or special occasion.

### PROS

- You own most of the items already.
- It's quick and easy to set up and take down.
- You can carry it in the smallest car or even on a motorcycle.
- It's a nice way to ease yourself, or your partner, into the idea of camping.
- You control the costs.

### CONS

- The tent may grant some privacy, but it doesn't protect against cold, rain, or bugs.
- Finding a private location can be difficult, but don't be tempted to trespass.
- Although you control the costs, they can climb more quickly than you expect. Fine foods and expensive champagne are usually the culprits.

## Elements of the Style

### LAYERS OF FABRIC

Pillows are piled on top of a vintage quilt. The tent is layers of fine netting, soft sheets, and colorful tablecloths draped over a strong cord.

### ENGAGE ALL THE SENSES

Finger foods, heady wine, and flowers conspire to pull you more firmly into the moment.

### SCENIC AND PRIVATE

Find a location that is beautiful in its own right and away from others and traffic noise.

# Essential Products

Flameless candles set the mood without the fire hazard. Being safe is being sexy.

If you're in an area where glass just isn't a good idea, but you crave sparkling wine, you can still bring it in a can.

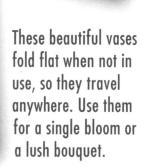

These beautiful vases fold flat when not in use, so they travel anywhere. Use them for a single bloom or a lush bouquet.

# Tips and Tricks for a
## *Romantic Picnic*

Food should be plated and set in your cooler before your guest arrives. If you do arrange it early, make sure it won't spoil and that it's covered.

All food should be bite-size and a mix of savory and sweet. Avoid food with strong flavors or smells.

A fun "rule" for your picnic is that you can't feed yourself, only each other, and you can't use flatware—fingers only.

Wine is fine.
Champagne is better.
But an elderflower
cocktail is
absolutely divine.

Have bottles of chilled
water stashed near
the tent. You'll want
them later.

Don't use bug spray on
your skin. Not only is it
poisonous, but it also
makes your tongue
go numb. Instead drape
a layer of netting or lace
over your entire tent to
keep the bugs out.

# DIY *Trysting Tent*

Although the tent doesn't need to stand up to the elements for several days, it does need to stand up for several hours. Nothing can ruin a romantic moment faster than having a tent collapse on you. Or getting cold and soaked from damp ground or light rain.

## 1

Place a 6 x 8 tarp on the ground. Next, layer rugs or blankets on top so that the tarp is covered.

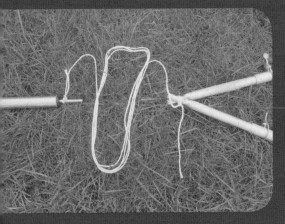

## 2

At one end of a 9-foot-long rope, tie two 5-foot poles together at the top. Tie the other end of the rope onto the top of a third pole.

# 3

Tie two 6-foot-long lengths of rope to the tops of the poles at each end. You'll need 4 lengths of rope. Tie the bottoms of the rope to ground stakes and stake them down.

# 4

On the other side, stretch the rope tying the poles until the rope is tight and the poles form an inverted V with the poles. Pound the ground stakes in until all the ropes are taut. If there is any slack in the ropes, the tent will collapse.

**5**

You can now layer lightweight sheets and tablecloths over the clothesline to make the tent. If you use netting or lace to keep the bugs out, use that as one of your first layers.

**6**

Add pillows and blankets to the inside and arrange. If you are worried about a light rain, you can layer a tarp between the netting and other fabrics so that it protects without being visible.

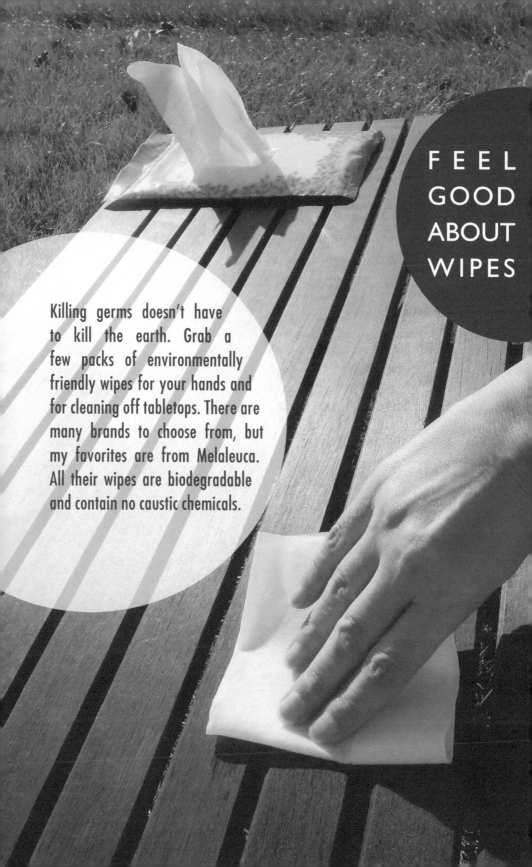

# FEEL GOOD ABOUT WIPES

Killing germs doesn't have to kill the earth. Grab a few packs of environmentally friendly wipes for your hands and for cleaning off tabletops. There are many brands to choose from, but my favorites are from Melaleuca. All their wipes are biodegradable and contain no caustic chemicals.

# Popping THE Question

While some may prefer the public nature of asking for their love's hand in marriage on the big screen at a major sporting event, others prefer a more romantic environment for such an important question. A fancy restaurant fits the bill for romance, but perhaps you want your intimate moment to be, well, more intimate. Create the perfect hidden nest for a romantic and memorable place to ask your beloved to spend the rest of their life with you.

Bring personal mementos with you. Hang a few photos of the two of you from a tree. The theme of this event is both of you, together, happily ever after.

If the theme is happily ever after, the focus is on your partner. What's your partner's favorite color? Use sheets and tablecloths that color. Favorite food? Favorite hobby? This is the moment to show you care for, and have paid careful attention to, your partner.

You want the scene to be perfect from the moment your partner lays eyes on it. The food should be out, but covered; the beverages chilled; and the table set. Have a friend set everything up while you escort your partner to the site.

Consider proposing in the evening, right as the sun is starting to set. Use groupings of flameless candles. Set them everywhere. A soft glow should surround the entire area.

Don't clean up or tear down the tent in front of your partner. When you're done, leave. Otherwise you destroy the fairy-tale spell you worked so hard to create. As you leave, text your secret helper to come and clean up the area for you. Be sure to leave them a gift with their name on it—appreciation is never a bad idea.

# ONE *Tent* THREE *Ways*

There is no specific style for a trysting tent, as we all have different preferences. If my husband did a Nebraska Husker football theme for our trysting tent and had the fight song playing, he'd be one very lucky man in a matter of moments. No accounting for taste, right? To help spark your own ideas, here are three more ways to style a trysting tent; each uses the same basic setup.

This is the fairy-tale bower. Reclaimed barn wood and long branches form the base of this tent; foliage and lilac branches fill in. Be sure to have a layer of fine netting or lace under the wood and flowers, or you'll be driven insane by bugs.

This Zen style calls for a more restrained hand in both number of objects and color palette. Woods, especially bamboo, with small splashes of black and green contribute to a serene, natural ambiance. The faux screen for the tent was created out of a white table cloth and black tape.

Combining elements of goth, neo-Victoriana, and a touch of the Industrial Revolution, steampunk is a fun and engaging style to play with. Whimsy rules the day, while the colors are browns and white with lace and brass accents. Go for a few bold touches rather than numerous small details.

# Choose the Best Campsite

With the trysting tent, privacy is the number-one consideration. Other times when you camp, if you do so at a campground, you may not get to pick where you pitch your tent. I try to camp at places where I can choose my spot. So what do I look for?

**A GOOD VIEW**

I like trees and don't like close neighbors, roads, and playgrounds. Don't camp by the toilets. Trust me. If there's a corner spot where I can be tucked away from everyone, that's where I want to be.

**HIGHER GROUND**

When it rains, and it almost always does, I don't want water running into my tent. You may have to put up with more wind higher up, but on the plus side it keeps the mosquitoes and bees away. You may prefer bees and water to possibly having the wind rip your tent down—your choice. I scream and run from bees like an idiot, so I just use heavy-duty stakes on my tent and call it good.

**HARD AND FLAT**

So many ways I could go with this. Ahem. You want a hard, flat surface to pitch your tent. Soft and lumpy is no good. Take the time to clear away rocks, sticks, and other debris from where you want to pitch your tent. If there's a slope, have your tent opening face downhill to prevent rain from coming in.

**SAFE AND SECURE**

Check around for signs of animals. Rocky ledges equal snakes, and garbage cans equal raccoons. Don't camp under trees that have a dead tree leaning against them. Look for poisonous plants and then don't camp there. Otherwise you'll walk right into the stuff when you have to pee at four a.m.

# *Floor Pillows* DIY

I love floor pillows. You can use them to add more seating almost anywhere. For a trysting tent, pile them inside the tent to use as seats during your romantic dinner. Floor pillows are among the easiest sewing projects, and once you make one, you'll want to make ten.

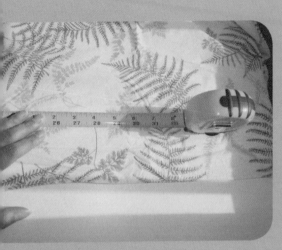

# 1

Choose from vinyl tablecloths, beach towels, or outdoor-rated fabrics. Cut two squares approximately 30 inches each.

# 2

Place the right sides of the fabric together and pin along all edges.

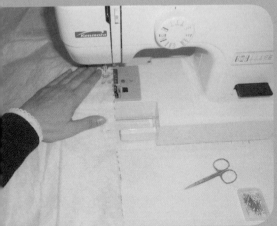

# 3

Sew along all 4 edges, leaving a 4-inch gap in the middle of one side.

**4**

Turn the pillow right-side out and use your finger or a pencil eraser end to poke the corners out.

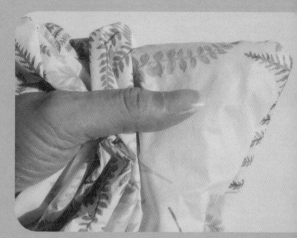

**5**

Stuff the pillow with fiberfill. This is a washable synthetic filling that dries quickly when wet.

**6**

Make as many of these pillows as you want. They don't have to match, and you can have a different pattern on each side of the pillow.

# Romantic
# Cocktails &
# Recipes

**CREAM CHEESE BITES**

# Wine and Cheese Pairings

There are thousands of different varieties of wine and cheese, which can make putting together a balanced combination a bit daunting. Wine snobs have done their best to suck the fun out of enjoying a glass of wine by making you worry you're Doing It Wrong. As long as you like the wine, you're fine. I'll give you a few suggestions, with the understanding that these are just suggestions. If you have personal preferences, go for it and enjoy!

- Sauvignon blanc goes well with goat, cheddar, and Stilton cheese.

- Pinot grigio goes well with Camembert, Swiss, and Boursin cheese.

- Syrah or Shiraz goes well with Brie, Maytag Blue, and Parmesan cheese.

- Pinot noir goes well with fresh mozzarella, Bonbel, and ubriaco cheese.

- Sweet champagne/sparkling wine goes well with mascarpone, Carmela, and La Peral cheese.

- Dry champagne doesn't go well with anything. That's my view, which you can happily ignore.

# Cream Cheese Bites

This dessert is so easy that anyone can make it and so rich and gooey that everyone will love it. Let's face it: With that much cream cheese and sugar, how can you go wrong?

## INGREDIENTS

1 box gluten-free yellow cake mix
1/2 cup butter, melted
3 eggs
1 8-ounce package of cream cheese, softened
1 ½ cups powdered sugar

## DIRECTIONS

Set oven to 350 degrees F.
Grease a 9 x 13 sheet pan.
Mix together the cake mix, butter, and 1 egg. The mixture will be crumbly. Press it into the bottom of the sheet pan.
In a bowl, mix the cream cheese, 2 eggs, and the powdered sugar.
Pour onto the top of the yellow cake mixture.
Bake for 20 minutes, or until a toothpick inserted into the center comes out clean.
Let cool and cut into bite-size bars, one inch square.

Optional: you can add berries to the bars by placing them gently into the cream cheese batter before baking.

# Portobello Pâté

• • • • • • • • • • • • • • • • • • • • • • • • • • • • • • • • •

Growing up in the rural Midwest, I wasn't exposed to vegan cuisine. It's still not my first choice. However, this pâté is one of my favorite recipes. Elegant truffle oil and earthy mushrooms—I'm drooling just thinking about it. Since it doesn't include ingredients that spoil easily, it's ideal for camping or picnics.

## INGREDIENTS

2 cups finely chopped
    portobello mushrooms
½ cup, mixed half and half,
    of almonds and cashews
2 tablespoons olive oil

3 bay leaves
2 cloves of garlic
1 cup dry white wine
1 teaspoon truffle oil
Salt and pepper to taste

## DIRECTIONS

Sauté mushrooms on medium in a covered pan with wine, bay leaves, and garlic for about 20 to 30 minutes. Liquid should thicken to a sauce, but don't allow to scorch or burn. While mushrooms are cooking, put nuts and olive oil in a food processor or a really good blender. Combine until you have a smooth paste.

When mushrooms are done, remove bay leaves and add to the nut paste and combine until mostly smooth.

Let cool for ten minutes and then add truffle oil. Add salt and pepper to taste.

Optional: If you plan on doing serious smooching, you can omit the garlic. Otherwise, keep the garlic, and add ¼ cup of minced onion while you're at it.

# Elderflower Flirtini

This cocktail takes champagne to a whole new level. I get the elderflower syrup from IKEA.

1 part vodka
1 part elderflower syrup
1 part grapefruit juice
½ part lemon juice
Splash of champagne

Shake the first 4 ingredients together in a shaker with ice. Strain into a flute and top with champagne.

Don't drink alcohol? No problem. Omit the vodka and substitute ginger ale for champagne. Can't drink grapefruit juice due to medication interactions? Try orange juice instead.

# Candied Flowers

Pretty to look at, sweet to eat. Use them as garnish on desserts, drop into a drink, or pop them into your mouth as a candy.

Edible flowers such as violets
1 egg white, beaten
¼ cup superfine sugar

Using a brush, paint a layer of egg white onto each side of the flowers. While still wet, place the flowers in a bag of sugar and very gently shake.
Remove flowers from bag and let dry for 8 hours. Store at room temperature in an airtight bag.

# MODERN
## minimalist

# MODERN MINIMALIST

When space or time is at a premium, but comfort is still desired, a sleek modern look is just the ticket. As in the Tiny House movement, careful consideration is given to organization and storage. Bold color and strong lines add style. This tent is my favorite of all the tents I have owned, and this setup is the one I most commonly use when camping. I may tinker with the accessories, like a new custom rain fly, but this is what I come back to. It's the perfect balance of comfort, style, and speed of setup. What can I say—I like red and brushed aluminum.

## PROS

- Can be stored in an apartment closet and fit in any car.
- Quick and easy to set up. I've done it in the dark. Drunk.
- Doesn't skimp on basics and still includes important comfort details.
- Very inexpensive. I paid thirty-four dollars for the tent.

## CONS

- You can't stand up in the tent. If you need to change your clothes inside it, I hope you're very flexible.
- One person is perfect in this four-person tent; two are cramped. A week could end a marriage.
- The kitchen prep-and-cooking table is very small and is also your dining table.

# Elements of the Style

## BOLD COLOR

Pick one powerful color and allow it to be front and center. Likewise, if you pick any patterns, go with ones that are bold or geometric.

## ARCHITECTURAL LINES

Treat the shapes of your gear like sculptures and display them. Pick furniture with exposed metals and woods.

## FEWER AND LESS

A modern look is the opposite of clutter. Pack away small items and choose ones with multiple uses.

# ESSENTIAL PRODUCTS

Made for keeping knitting supplies organized, this works equally well in keeping your bedside materials neat and at hand.

This camp organizer clamps onto a table or can be staked into the ground. It holds a garbage bag and paper towels, and has hooks for pans, oven mitts, and cooking utensils.

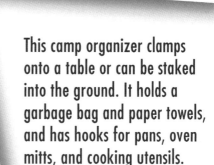

Fans are a great way to beat the heat, and this battery-operated fan works even when you don't have access to electricity.

# TIPS AND TRICKS FOR
## keeping electronics safe

Direct sunlight on hot days can kill your electronics. During the day, keep them somewhere shady and well ventilated.

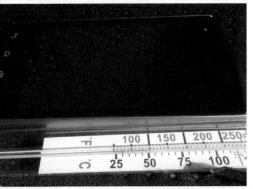

Locking your phone in the car may secure it from theft, but don't keep electronics there. On an 80-degree day, the temperature inside your car can climb to over 100 degrees in half an hour.

Excessive humidity and morning dew can also harm your electronics. A simple solution is place your e-reader in a sealed plastic bag. It stays safe, and you can still use it.

FEEL
GOOD
ABOUT
YOUR
STOVE

The BioLite CampStove is a compact stove that converts heat to electricity to charge small electronics via a USB port. It burns renewable resources like sticks and pinecones instead of using gas canisters and produces 90% less smoke than a typical wood fire. If that isn't amazing enough, your purchase helps bring safe, clean energy to families across the developing world with their larger format HomeStove.

# GIRLS' (or Guys')
# WEEKEND

In the right company, a few days out in the woods can make you feel as lighthearted as a kid again. So why not relive part of your childhood in a more adult way? Glamping Scouts is something my friends and I came up with, and we can't wait to earn our badges.

You can use some of our ideas or come up with badges that have special meaning for you and your friends.

Make simple sashes out of a sturdy material such as canvas or denim. You can find patterns on the internet.

Come up with fun badges to earn. Were you able to sleep past 10:00 a.m.? Make a perfect cocktail? Kill a spider without screaming? You deserve a badge.

So what's the easiest way to make badges? Find images and photos that represent badge-worthy accomplishments and then print them on iron-on transfer paper. Following the manufacturer's directions, iron them onto craft felt, cut them out into circles, and take them with you. If you bring fabric glue or a needle and thread you can apply them onto sashes or t-shirts while camping.

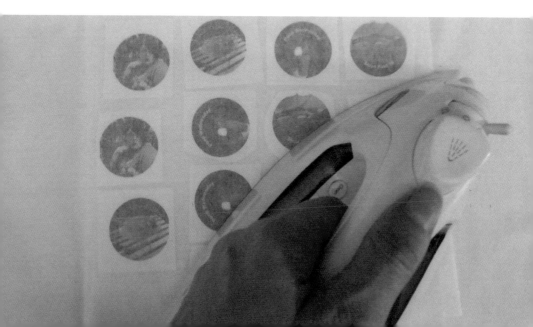

# DIY Rain Fly

You may have a perfectly serviceable rain fly, or you may have one that leaks like a sieve. Don't throw a great tent away because you hate the rain fly; make your own. Changing your rain fly can dramatically change the look of your entire campsite. This isn't for beginning sewers; it's an advanced project. If you don't know what a felled seam is, hire someone to make your rain fly for you.

The best fabrics for a rain fly are washable silks and nylon that feels similar to your original rain fly. You can use other fabrics, such as canvas or cotton sheets, but they will not fit back into your tent case.

Buy enough fabric to cover your rain fly 1.5 times. If there is a large pattern, you'll need more fabric to match the pattern. That's also far more difficult.

**1**

Set up your tent and your rain fly. You'll be using it to make a pattern.

**2**

Tape small pieces of paper on each section of the rain fly to number each section.

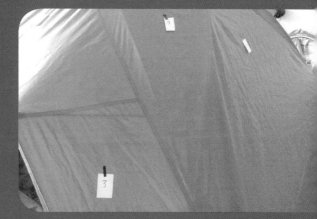

**3**

Lay a sheet of tissue paper on top of a section of the rain fly. Outline the shape of each section in pencil. Add 1 full inch to the outside of each outlined rain-fly section for seam allowance, and cut out the tissue-paper pieces. Number your pieces to match your drawing.

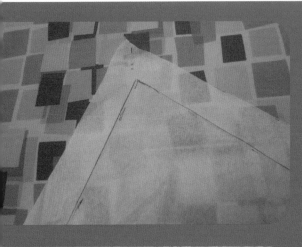

**4**

Pin the pieces of tissue-paper pattern to your fabric, paying attention to the fabric's pattern and how it will match up. (Think of it like a puzzle.) Cut it out.

**5**

You are now ready to assemble your rain fly. With right sides together, sew the two largest center pieces together using a felled seam.

**6**

Continue sewing new sections of the rain fly together, placing the new rain fly on the old one to check the fit after each section and making adjustments.

**7**

Use a synthetic finishing tape or long strips of the fabric to cover the entire outside edge of the rain fly.

**8**

Lay the finished rain fly outside or in a well-ventilated place. Spray the entire rain fly with 3 thin coats of tent sealer, on both sides, allowing time for drying between coats.

**9**

Buy clamping tarp bungees to tie the rain fly down. Depending on your tent, you'll either stake them to the ground or attach them to your tent with a hook.

# — CHOOSE THE BEST TENT —

T he best tent for me may not be the best tent for you. My favorite tent for a weekend isn't the one I'd pick for a week. A tent shelters you from the elements and protects you from critters. If it rains, you'll spend more time in it than you may have planned. There are all kinds of tents out there, so what one is best for you?

**YOUR BUDGET**

Estimate how much you can spend, then decide if you want a new or used tent. If you go used, you can afford a higher-quality tent. If you buy new, you're assured there aren't any holes or broken poles, or if there is something wrong, you can exchange the tent for a new one. Also, read the online reviews and testimonials —don't just look at the number of stars.

**NUMBER OF PEOPLE**

To phrase this politely, tent manufacturers stretch the truth on how many people fit in their tents. My small red tent is rated to hold four people. I have no idea how four people could sleep in my tent unless we slept sitting up like soldiers in a foxhole. The tent is perfect for me and my gear or me and my husband with our gear outside. A general rule of thumb is whatever occupancy is listed, divide by half to three-quarters.

**DURATION VS. SPEED**

Pay attention to how the tent sets up. The more poles, the harder it is to set up. However, easy isn't always better. The number-one complaint I hear from people about their tent is that they can't stand up and move around in it. I have a tent that takes my husband and me forty-five minutes to set up. The tent is obviously designed for people with advanced engineering degrees, but the extra room is worth the setup time. The number-two complaint I hear from people is that their tent takes too long to set up. Find your balance.

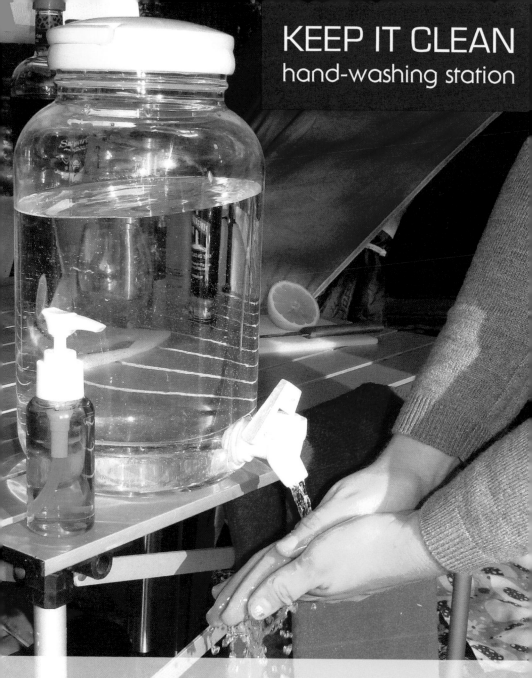

# KEEP IT CLEAN
## hand-washing station

I hate being dirty, and one of the things that sends me into immediate bitch mode is not being able to easily wash my hands. Hiking over to the communal water spigot every time doesn't improve my mood, either. Now that I have a hand-washing station, life is good. To set one up, get a plastic beverage container and fill it with water. Set pump soap and a hand towel next to it, and voilà! It's also nice for brushing your teeth after every meal. Being in the woods is no excuse for poor dental hygiene.

# ONE table

## THREE ways

Today's disposable tableware has come a long way from the plain white paper plates most of us grew up with. You can now create a fine alfresco dining experience without the cleanup and breakage problems of real china and glass. I broke several wineglasses over the years before I figured out that klutzy people who drink alcohol shouldn't use glass when camping. If you'd rather not use disposable products, there are other camping-friendly options. Mix it up and have fun!

A very bright take on cottage-style dining, this look is inspired by the tablecloth by Marimekko. The plates are paperware, and the "silverware" is disposable plastic. Mason jars would suit cottage style, but I opted for lead-free pewter wineglasses found at a garage sale.

Asian influence and a modern aesthetic go well together and work well for camping. This look is all about shapes and contrasts. The table runner, which is wrapping paper, highlights the place settings and the exposed metal of the table. The plates are dishwasher-safe plastic, while the napkins and cups are disposable.

Formal without being stuffy, the plates are heavy-duty paper with matching napkins. The wineglasses are an unbreakable polycarbonate, and I've put them to the test. The flatware is brass and ebony from an estate sale. The best part? When dinner is over, I roll the disposables up in the plastic-backed paper tablecloth and toss it in the garbage.

# keep it organized:

# BINS

Stackable plastic bins make camping so much easier. Plastic bins protect your items from rain, humidity, and animals. Look for bins that can be snapped or clamped shut. Raccoons have thumbs; this at least makes trying to get into your gear challenging for them.

Group your gear in bins so that everything is easy to find. Your tools go in one bin, kitchen items in another, clothes in a third. Make sure you color-code your bins, have clear bins, or label your bins in some way. Every time you take something out of a bin, once you're done using it, put it back! I know, I sound like my dad, but he was right. The real magic of plastic bins happens when you get home. Clean out your bins, restock or replace any missing or damaged items, and then store them with your other camping gear. Next time you want to go camping, all you need to do is grab your bins and go.

# keep it safe

## FIRST AID KIT

There's one camping rule I'm hardcore about; always bring a first aid kit and hang it where you can quickly access it. At a minimum, your kit should include antiseptic wipes, antibacterial ointment, poison oak/ivy cream, a variety of self-adhesive bandages, nonstick sterile pads, medical tape, blister pads, antihistamine for allergic reactions, tweezers to remove splinters, a first aid manual or information cards, and a card with your emergency information, including insurance, allergies, blood type, and emergency contact information.

# KEEP IT EASY: beverages

Sure, you can bring a French press, ground coffee, a teapot, loose tea leaves, a strainer, assorted liquors, mixers, and juices. But you don't need to. These premixed and instant beverages cut down on what you need to pack and make getting a good drink easier and quicker. A premium cosmo or margarita can be in your glass in seconds. Instant coffee is still quick but without the instant taste. Hot or chilled tea, with honey, now comes in a powder you pour into a water bottle, shake, and drink.

# CONVENIENT
## COCKTAILS **&** RECIPES

**BLACKBERRY, FENNEL, & GOAT CHEESE PIZZA**

# Upgrading Ready-to-Serve Cocktails

Each year there are more types of cocktail in a bottle. All you do is open the bottle and pour the contents into a glass. The good news is that most of these cocktails no longer taste like crap. In fact, a few are downright OK. If OK isn't good enough for you, they can be upgraded to mighty tasty with minimal time and effort.

**BASIC UPGRADE** Garnish the drink with fresh fruit. If the drink is a grapefruit margarita, place a thin slice of grapefruit, with the peel, in the glass. You want the oil from the peel, not only the juice from the fruit, to liven up the cocktail.

**ADVANCED UPGRADE** Add a complementary herb to the drink. Muddle the herb in the glass before you pour in the cocktail. Some herbs are so delicate that throwing in the ice cubes is enough to bruise the leaves and release the flavors. Looking again at our grapefruit margarita, lightly muddle a small sprig of rosemary or tarragon.

Not sure what herbs go with specific fruits? Here's a short list of optimal pairings:

Strawberry and Basil

Pineapple and Mint

Kiwi and Thyme

Blackberry and Oregano

Cucumber and Cilantro

Pink Grapefruit and Tarragon

Green Apple and Parsley

# Blackberry, Fennel, and Goat Cheese Pizza

I know—fruit on your pizza? Well, tomatoes are fruit, and most of us enjoy them on pizza. Healthier, tastier, and just as easy to make as a pepperoni pizza, this recipe will become a camping favorite. Options are given below for vegan and gluten-free versions.

## INGREDIENTS

1 prepared pizza crust
1 tablespoon olive oil
1 ½ cups fresh or frozen (thawed) blackberries
1 small fennel bulb, thinly sliced
8 ounces goat cheese (or Brie)
2 tablespoons fresh thyme
1 tablespoon honey
Salt and pepper to taste

## DIRECTIONS

Set your cooking tripod or grill over a fire with a good bed of coals, but no high flames.
Drizzle olive oil over pizza crust.
Add berries, fennel, cheese, and thyme to crust.
Place on the grill or tripod over the fire for 8 to 12 minutes, or until the cheese is melted—whichever is longer.
Top with honey before serving.

Optional: You can easily make this gluten-free by purchasing a gluten-free pizza crust. If you'd prefer the pizza to be vegan, substitute a vegan cashew "cheese" for the goat cheese and use agave in place of honey.

# Fresh Salsa

Salsa is great as a snack or a topping for main dishes, but don't use store-bought salsa. Making your own is easy and cheap, and tastes so much better. Make a large batch at home and stick it in your cooler.

## INGREDIENTS

2 14.5-ounce cans diced tomatoes
1 bunch fresh cilantro
½ yellow or red onion, finely chopped
2 jalapeños, seeded, very finely diced
Optional: 1 clove of garlic, pressed
Salt to taste

## DIRECTIONS

Place 1 can of tomatoes and the cilantro bunch into a blender or processor and coarsely puree. Pour puree into a bowl. Add in remaining can of diced tomatoes, onion, garlic, and jalapeños. Mix together. Add salt to taste.

# Banana Boats

These are simple to make, and the durable ingredients are great for camping. The bananas and marshmallows can be stored in the shade, but put the chocolate chips in your cooler.

A banana for each person
Mini marshmallows
Chocolate chips

Split the banana skin along the fruit's inner curve. Stuff the marshmallows and chocolate chips into the banana and wrap the banana up in foil. Place it on a grill over the campfire for 8 minutes. Enjoy!

# Pot Roast Dinner

Pot roast is one of the easiest dinners to make and the easiest to screw up. This recipe will give you perfect pot roast every time. For camping, I like to freeze the meat and place it in my cooler in a sealed bag. Halfway through a week-long camping trip, the meat is thawed out and I'm ready for a super-easy dinner.

## INGREDIENTS

Beef pot roast; plan on 1 pound per person
1 can of cream of mushroom soup
2 medium, quartered potatoes or 6 small whole potatoes
  per person
½ onion per person, roughly chopped
2 carrots per person, peeled, cut into 4 pieces
1 clove garlic, chopped (optional)
Water
Salt and pepper to taste

## DIRECTIONS

Place fully thawed pot roast in a Dutch oven or a roasting pan. Pour in water until it is one inch deep, the add in can of soup.
Throw in everything else. If you like firmer carrots, wait to add them 1 hour before serving.
Cover and cook over a low-burning fire on a tripod for at least 6 hours.

Note: If you are cooking the roast all day on a tripod over a fire, there are times you'll have to add wood and the fire will burn higher and hotter. During those times I raise the tripod. When the fire burns down, I lower it. Tender roasts require longer cooking times at lower temperatures.

# Serene
# SAFARI

# SERENE SAFARI

*T*his camp setup isn't for those who like to camp light, but you can still load it into an average-size car. I was able to get everything into my Yaris, but I couldn't see out any of the side or back windows. That probably wasn't legal, so don't do that. Next to shabby chic, the safari look is a favorite of glampers. Tailored enough to appeal to both men and women, it screams pampering and sophistication - but screams it in a very genteel way.

## PROS

- If pieces are picked carefully, you can pack it into most cars, but a SUV would be best.
- High impact visually, high degree of comfort, high quality.
- Canopy tents, with sides, have come down in price. Watch for sales and you can find one for fifty dollars.
- Setup time is under half an hour for two people.

## CONS

- Most canopy tents do not have a floor. This means bugs and animals can enter your tent. Hanging mosquito netting can help.
- This look can be one false step from looking junky. Everything must remain spotless, and exercise restraint when choosing accessories.
- While the tent may be inexpensive, the accessories often aren't.

## ELEMENTS OF THE STYLE

### RESTRAINT

I've seen some safari set-ups use indigenous prints, but the campsites were arranged by professional interior designers with budgets above $10,000. The rest of us should stick to one statement piece such as a backdrop in a single color.

### LOOK TO THE BRITS

The Brits knew how to camp in style during the mid-1800s. Your accessories should emulate theirs and be of heirloom quality.

### TAILORED

Look for pieces that are more masculine. The bedding pictured here is charcoal-gray cashmere, like a fine men's suit.

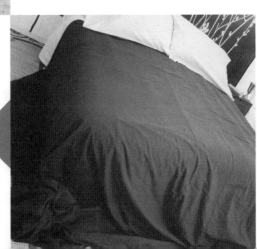

# ESSENTIAL PRODUCTS

This bar is a replica of ones used on the grand tours of Egypt and India in the mid-1800s.

This shaving and washing stand is made from wrought iron and comes apart in three pieces for easy transport.

A tripod is one of the more versatile tools for cooking your food. The cooking surface can be raised and lowered.

# TIPS AND TRICKS FOR
## *setting up a kitchen*

Traditional camp kitchens have one fatal flaw: they are too low. For a kitchen work surface that is countertop height, use an ironing board or folding table that adjusts to the proper height.

Keep your cooler in the shade. Drape a tablecloth over your kitchen work area and store coolers there.

A shower organizer makes a handy pantry for dry goods and cooking supplies.

Plan how you will wash dishes. Two small bins and a flat-pack drying rack make the job easier.

Bring two good knives and a cutting board. A serrated knife and a larger chopping knife should be all you need.

Print your recipes and place them in a photo stand. The sleeves protect the recipes, and the stand makes it all hands-free.

# KEEP IT CLEAN
## *pop-up garbage can*

While some camping places provide communal garbage cans, others don't. And remember my tip to not pitch your tent near the permanent garbage cans? Bees swarm them during the day, and raccoons visit at night. This garbage can packs flat and pops open to use. Just line it with a garbage bag and empty it every night before you go to bed. You can find garbage cans like this in the lawn-care section of home improvement stores.

# keep it safe

## FIRE SAFE GLOVES

A cozy campfire. Making a delicious breakfast on a camp stove. These activities create some of your favorite memories, but they can also create something else - burns. To stay safe, invest in a good pair of fire safe gloves. These gloves protect your hands and lower arms while you add wood to a fire or remove a hot pan from the stove. Plus, they work well as trivets. You can find them where fireplace accessories are sold such as Walmart, Target, or Kmart.

# DIY *Ice Chest Renovation*

Coolers work well for foods that can be frozen or can get wet. My food desires run wider than that, so I take both a cooler and an ice chest. An ice chest stands upright, has shelves, and has a solid block of ice with a drip pan. If you want to take dairy, herbs, or fruits and vegetables camping, you'll want to find an old ice chest and renovate it.

**1** Clean the inside and outside of the ice chest with a mild soap. If there are any holes, seal them with a food-safe caulk.

**2** If the ice-block holder and drip pan are missing, purchase two small plastic bins. One should be deeper than the other. Poke holes in the bottom of the shallow pan and fill the deeper pan ¾ full of water and freeze. This makes the perfect block of ice.

If the ice chest is missing the shelves, measure the width and depth of the ice chest. That's how big your shelf needs to be. You can either find plastic trays that match the width, or you can cut thin wood sheets to size.

Place the ice block in the shallow pan, nested in the deeper pan so that the water from the ice can drip into the larger pan. Remember— water is the enemy of ice.

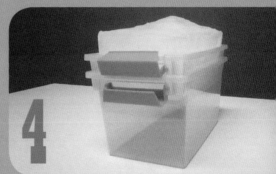

Place ice block in the bottom of the chest and load up your shelves. Place dairy and eggs closer to the ice, herbs farther away. Your ice chest may have originally had the ice bin at the top since cold air flows down, but there's a reason most ice chests have broken or missing shelves and ice bins: the weight of the ice was too much.

# *Host a* SYMPOSIA

*L*eave it to academics to suck the fun out of what was a wild night with friends. Symposia, in ancient Greece, were drinking parties with a specific purpose—to strengthen the bonds of friendship. I've hosted parties and I've hosted symposia, and nothing beats symposia for friendship and fun. Nothing.

You want to have between ten and fourteen guests at a symposium. That's enough people to keep the conversation rolling but not so many that several smaller conversations form instead of one large conversation.

Conversation and flowing wine are key to a successful symposium. Pick a few people you know well, a few people you barely know, and a few people you wish to know. Above all, pick interesting people. Then pamper them.

The meal is leisurely; serve one course, with wine pairings, every twenty minutes for a total of six courses: appetizer, soup, fish, main, fine vegetable or salad, dessert.

There is no way around this: your guests will get drunk. That's the purpose of symposia—to erase normal social barriers but to do so in a structured environment. Symposia have rules, and they must be followed:

- All guests are to strive for harmony. You can disagree but you can't be disagreeable. It's the host's job to remind guests of this, if needed.

- A new topic is introduced for each course. Mix it up between serious and silly topics; you'll learn more about one another that way.

- The host doesn't need to do all the cooking or supply all the wine. Guests can form two-person teams that are each responsible for a course.

- Use tablecloths, pretty paperware, flowers—anything that makes your guests feel special. The food and wine should be just as special.

- When the symposium dinner is done, the guests leave. They don't stay around and party afterward.

Hosting a six-course dinner for twelve people while camping may seem daunting, but the results are worth it. Almost every person I've ever invited to a symposium while camping has told me it was one of the most memorable experiences they've ever had. I've become close friends with people I barely knew until I invited them to symposia. Try it and then let me know how it went.

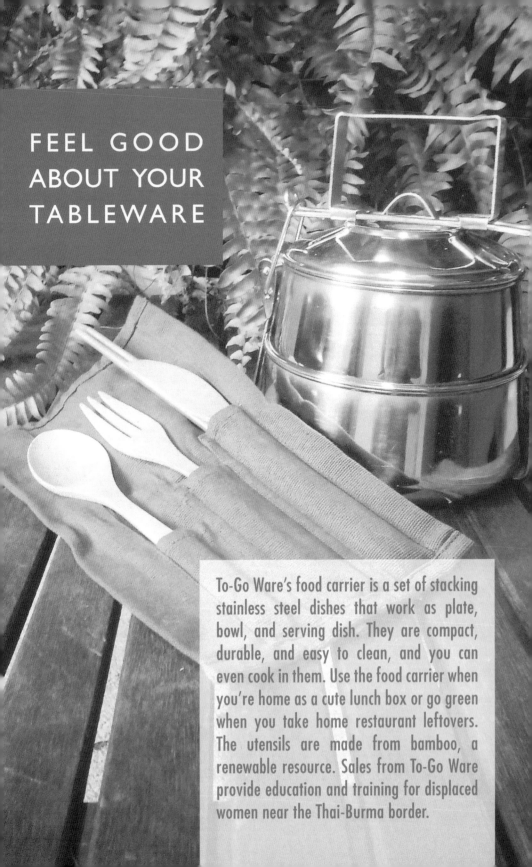

# FEEL GOOD ABOUT YOUR TABLEWARE

To-Go Ware's food carrier is a set of stacking stainless steel dishes that work as plate, bowl, and serving dish. They are compact, durable, and easy to clean, and you can even cook in them. Use the food carrier when you're home as a cute lunch box or go green when you take home restaurant leftovers. The utensils are made from bamboo, a renewable resource. Sales from To-Go Ware provide education and training for displaced women near the Thai-Burma border.

# CHOOSE THE BEST CAMPSITE

You don't realize how many different types of camp stoves there are until you start to look. Each has its charms and challenges, and getting the right one for you depends on your cooking style, ability level, and desired ecological footprint.

### WHAT'S MOST IMPORTANT

If you want to make scones while a pan of bacon is frying and coffee is percolating, you'll want a stove/oven combination. This gives you the greatest versatility. If you just need to heat up a can of something, look for a one-burner butane stove. They're handy and cheap, but the flame adjustments aren't that sensitive. A step up is a multiburner propane model, but don't get a cheap one; you'll regret it. If grilling lots of meat or cooking stews, purchase a sturdy adjustable tripod. Next to the stove/oven combination, this is your most versatile option.

### HOW TALENTED ARE YOU

If you strictly follow recipes when cooking, choose a multiburner propane camp stove or splurge and buy a stove/oven combination. Both these choices have easy to understand temperature settings that take the guesswork out of cooking. If you cook by look or feel, you'll enjoy the woodburning options, such as the tripod or a BioLite. With no temperature gauges, cooking becomes an art, rather than a science.

### FOOTPRINT

Are you trying to be more green? Packing in and packing out? Opt for a BioLite or solid fuel tabs. Have more money and space? Pick the stove/oven. Have the space but not the money? A tripod is the best option. In an area where there is a danger of starting a fire? The propane or butane burners, if used carefully, are the safer options.

# ONE *lunch* THREE *ways*

Whether it's hot or cold outside, a ploughman's lunch hits the spot. It's easy to throw together, appealing to look at, and impossible to get sick of because there are so many variations. I'm torturing myself by including bread as the basic part of the lunch—a hunk of really good, crusty bread is off-limits to me as I have celiac disease. Yes, I know there are gluten-free breads, but as of yet, they are nothing I'd voluntarily put in my mouth. Perhaps someday . . .

A lightly smoked fish paired with a small salad of mixed greens. The salad is really just an excuse to pour on an excellent homemade vinaigrette. You'll mop that up with the bread, slathered in a soft cheese.

Scoop up the hummus with the bread and top with the marinated, grilled, chilled veggies. The olives add something salty, while the dried fruit provides the sweet. The nuts? They add a bit of crunch. This lunch will please both vegans and non-vegans.

If you need a more substantial lunch, look to this German-inspired fare. Layer coarse-ground mustard, smooth braunschweiger, and hard yellow cheese onto bites of the bread. The pickles and hardboiled eggs complement the other earthy flavors without being too much the same.

# KEEP IT EASY:
## *packaged herbs*

*H*erbs lift your meals from OK to awesome, but taking the bottles of herbs from your kitchen isn't always practical, as humidity can ruin an entire bottle or canister. That's wasteful and expensive. Or maybe you want fresh herbs and don't want all the fuss that fresh herb care requires. There are frozen and dry herbs you can buy in packaged, premeasured amounts. Just pop them into your cooler or your kitchen food-prep bin and go.

# KEEP IT ORGANIZED:
## *cooler*

Coolers aren't exactly huge, yet it's amazing how much stuff can get lost in them. Where are the sliced meats? I just saw them when I was looking for a beer. And so on for your entire trip. Organize your cooler, and you won't have this problem. If you can, bring two coolers—one for drinks and one for food. In your food cooler, use plastic and waterproof food containers and label the top of each with what's inside. If you want bonus points, you can color code them. Stack them up, and you won't lose your blue-cheese stuffed dates again.

# DIY *Frozen & Fresh Herbs*

Using fresh herbs makes any meal tastier, but unless you have an ice chest, like the one featured earlier, they're tricky to bring camping. Freezing your own herbs is easy and insures your herbs are fresh.

**1**

Herbs that freeze well include basil, chives, cilantro, garlic, mint, parsley, rosemary, sage, and thyme. Wash herbs and gently pat dry.

**2**

If herbs are on a stem, remove the leaves. Finely mince the leaves and add a small amount of cooking oil, just enough that they form a clump.

**3**

Measure herbs into 1-tea-spoon balls and place on a sealing type of plastic wrap and seal them in little bubbles. Place in the freezer in labeled sandwich bags.

**4**

If you need fresh herbs without the oil, one solution is to bring them on the stem and place them in a cup of water.

**5**

An attractive way way to enjoy fresh herbs while camping it to bring them in a small planter. Just snip off what you need.

# Herb-Infused Cocktails

**SAGE LADY**

# HOT MULLED PINEAPPLE CIDER

If you're looking for a drink to sip while snuggled in a blanket gazing into the campfire, this is it.
Enjoy it with or without the rum.

½ gallon apple cider
8 cinnamon sticks
8 star anise
4 cups pineapple juice
1 ounce rum per serving

In a large saucepan combine cider, cinnamon, and star anise and bring to a simmer. Reduce heat and simmer 5 minutes. Pour into mugs and add the rum.

# SAGE LADY

Very simple, and even people who don't like gin enjoy this drink. Sage leaves are among the more durable fresh herbs, which makes them a good choice for camping.

2 parts gin
¾ part lemon juice
¾ part simple syrup
2 sage leaves

In a shaker, lightly bruise one of the sage leaves.
Add gin, lemon juice, and simple syrup.
Shake with a few ice cubes. Strain into a glass and garnish with a "spanked" sage leaf (to release the oils).

# GIN GARDEN

Fresh and light, the cilantro and grapefruit brighten up the gin. Don't leave off the cucumber slice; it's part of the charm. If you're one of the unlucky people who can't stand cilantro, try tarragon instead.

2 parts gin
1 part grapefruit juice
½ part cilantro simple syrup
¼ part lime juice
Garnish with cucumber slice

Shake the first 4 ingredients together in a shaker with ice. Strain into a tall glass with ice and garnish with the slice of cucumber.

## Cilantro Simple Syrup

Make this at home before you hit the trail.
- In a small pan, gently heat 1 cup of water and 1 cup of sugar until sugar is completely dissolved.
- Remove from heat, pour into a glass jar, and allow to cool.
- Add a good-sized handful of fresh cilantro leaves to the jar. Seal the top and store in the fridge overnight.
- The next day, strain out the cilantro leaves and put the syrup in a clean, sealed jar. The syrup will keep for up to 2 weeks in the fridge and can be frozen.

## Tarragon Simple Syrup

In a small saucepan, combine the sugar and water over medium heat, stirring until the sugar has dissolved. Add 4 tablespoons of tarragon leaves, turn off the heat, and steep for 10 minutes. Strain, and store in a glass jar in the fridge.

# LAVENDER LEMONADE

I like everything about this drink: the smell, the taste, the color. With or without alcohol, this cocktail is pure summer.

1 part vodka
1 part lavender simple syrup
2 parts lemonade

Shake all ingredients together in a shaker with ice. Strain into a tall glass filled with ice.

### Lavender Simple Syrup

In a small saucepan, combine 2 cups sugar and 2 cups water over medium heat, stirring until the sugar has dissolved. Add 1 cup food-grade lavender blossoms. Turn off the heat and steep for 10 minutes. Strain, and store in a glass jar in the fridge.

# VARIATION: LAVENDER MARTINI

If you like your drinks a bit more dry, or you're looking for a sophisticated evening cocktail, make a lavender martini. In a shaker, put 2 parts vodka and 1 part lavender simple syrup. Shake with ice until well chilled; strain into a martini glass. Garnish with a twist of lemon.

## SAFFRON MARGARITA

The addition of saffron threads and the unusual base of mango transport you to paradise. Be warned: these margaritas are like potato chips—no one can have just one.

1 part tequila
½ part Cointreau
½ part lime juice
2 parts mango puree or mango juice
1 teaspoon agave
Very small pinch of saffron threads

Shake all ingredients together in a shaker with ice. Strain into a lowball glass. The saffron threads will float to the top.

## FALL APPLE

Refreshing and light any time of year, this cocktail is especially tasty on warm fall afternoons. Make it by the pitcher and share with friends.

1 bottle sparkling wine, sweet or semi-sweet
6 Tbsp. Calvados
1 small bottle sparkling apple cider, hard or non-alcoholic
1 small sprig of fresh rosemary per person

Pour all well chilled liquids into a pitcher and give a light stir. In each glass, place a lightly bruised sprig or rosemary, then top with the beverage.

# Delightful
# DECADE

# DELIGHTFUL DECADE

I f you've been into glamping at all, you'll have seen countless versions of fifties style. That's not my thing. I love the seventies. The seventies had less innocence and more fun than the fifties, and more cynicism and less pot than the sixties. Plus, earth tones and fall colors were all the rage, and that's the color palette I prefer. This setup is for a family or a group of people camping together. It assumes you have access to electricity and water at your campsite. It also assumes you have a larger vehicle because this is a whole lotta gear.

## PROS

- Lots of room to spread out, and if it rains, you'll still have a great time.
- Separate rooms in the tent mean that small children can nap or go to bed earlier without being woken up by parents moving around.
- You have your own shower. And air conditioner. And kitchen. And dining room. What's not to love?

## CONS

- I hope you have a strong relationship, because tents this large are complicated to set up, and it'll take you about two hours to get the whole campsite put up.
- Expensive. From the tent, to the tons of gear, to the gas for the large vehicle you'll need to haul everything.

# *Elements of the Style*

## CONTRADICTION

The seventies is a fun decade to re-create because it was full of such contradictions: austerity and decadence, hippies and high-tech, disco and punk.

## BASE OF DRAB WITH EXPLOSIONS OF COLOR

When we think of the seventies, we think of avocado green, harvest gold, and wood-tone brown. Those were base colors, with Technicolor rainbow hues thrown on top. Forget a splash of color—let color explode.

## OPEN AND FAMILY FOCUSED

The seventies brought the family together in every room of the house, and the floor plans of homes opened up. Do the same with your campsite and make family activities in shared space your focus.

# ESSENTIAL PRODUCTS

Scour secondhand stores for a retro suitcase bar and outfit it for the ultimate seventies drink, the Black Russian.

Gravity loungers fold up flat and deliver insane amounts of comfort. Sit up straight or kick back and nap.

Large, sturdy canopies allow you to enjoy being outside and use your kitchen whether the day is rainy or sunny and hot.

# TIPS AND TRICKS FOR ✦✦✦✦✦✦✦✦✦✦✦✦✦
## *family camping*

Have an area set aside for outdoor toys. This can be a kiddie corral or a sheet on the ground. Kids can play with the toys there or elsewhere, but that's where the toys get returned.

In case it rains, bring a few indoor activities, such as crayons and coloring books, homemade play-dough that can be thrown out if it gets dirty, card games, and small toys.

Place snacks in a bright-colored food container in the cooler or on the table. These are approved snacks that the kids know they can eat at any time.

Kids need to move around, so plan 2 physical activities per day. Go for a walk in the morning and swimming in the afternoon. Or a horseback ride. Or a game of Frisbee.

Your kids will get dirty. Don't freak out. Just hose them down once a day and wash their faces and hands before meals and bedtime.

Pack each day of your children's clothes in a gallon-size bag. Your child can grab a bag in the morning, get dressed, and stuff the dirty clothes back into the bag.

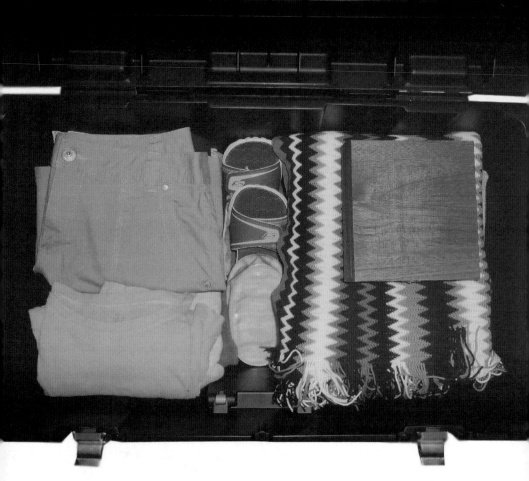

# KEEP IT ORGANIZED:
## clothes

nlike at home, there aren't closets or dressers in a tent. No laundry room, either. You can keep your clothes organized and accessible in your tent using a footlocker-style plastic bin. Place outfits for each day in one side of the bin. Add in a few sweatshirts or pullovers on the other side, along with your toiletry bag. If there's room, you can tuck an extra blanket in the bin. For added freshness, place a thin cedar board or a sachet of your favorite fragrance on the bottom of your bin.

# KEEP IT SAFE
## *the big three*

At a festival I attend each year, the organizers stress the big three in camping safety: water, sunscreen, and hard-soled shoes. Each day at the morning meeting, Selena Fox or someone from the safety committee says, "And remember . . ." and we all chant back, "Water, sunscreen, hard-soled shoes." That's some of the best commonsense camping safety information you'll ever get. Drink plenty of water; it's very easy to get dehydrated. If you aren't peeing every two hours, you aren't drinking enough water. Sunburn is an annoyance at home, where you can just go inside if you're getting too much sun; it's a serious problem while camping, where heat makes it impossible to stay in a tent during the day. Hard-soled shoes protect your feet from sticks, broken glass hidden in dirt, sharp rocks, and biting and stinging insects and animals. So remember . . . WATER, SUNSCREEN, HARD-SOLED SHOES.

4.2 oz / 120 g

# DIY *Drop Cloth Rug*

Rugs are a necessity when camping, and I bring several. Place one under your chairs to keep the bugs down. Put another outside the entrance of your tent to limit the amount of dirt you track inside the tent. Place a third inside your tent to trap the rest of the dirt and provide an insulating layer between you and the ground. Camping rugs should pack up small and should be inexpensive, easy to clean, and quick to dry; a drop cloth makes a perfect camping rug.

Decide what kind of pattern you'd like to have on the rug. If you want stripes or squares, you can make them with tape. If you want a more ornate pattern, you may have to find or create a stencil.

**1**

Buy a drop cloth the size you want your rug to be. Make sure it's a canvas or cotton duck drop cloth. Lay it out flat somewhere outside or in a garage.

**2**

Spray the entire back surface of the drop cloth with tent sealer or some type of fabric sealer. Let fully dry, about 2 hours, then do a second coat.

**3**

Using a foam roller, paint the entire rug with a base coat of latex paint. It should be the lightest of the colors you're planning on using. Let dry overnight.

**4**

If you are making stripes or geometric patterns, use painters tape to cover the areas you want blocked off from the next layer of paint. If using a stencil, use a pencil to trace the pattern onto the canvas.

**5**

Paint the second color over the top using a paint brush. Don't use too much paint, or it will bleed under the edges of the tape. Wait one hour and then pull the tape off.

## 6

If needed, you can touch up any rough edges or areas where the paint bled through using an art brush. It doesn't need to be perfect, just look for major problem areas.

## 7

When paint is completely dry, spray on another 2 layers of tent sealer spray and let dry overnight.

# YOU'RE DONE!

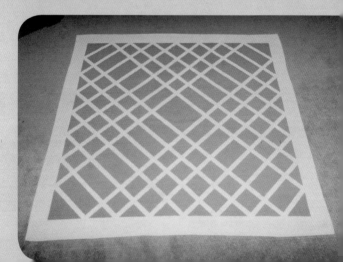

# CHOOSE THE BEST BED

Getting a good night's sleep can be an elusive quest for many people under the best of conditions, so finding the right bed and bedding is a priority. Try to find a bed that replicates, as closely as possible, the firmness level of your bed at home. Another tip that helps: bring your normal bedding or, at the very least, your pillow.

**FOAM MATTRESS**

These mattresses are basically thin foam bedrolls. The are nicely compact, and you don't have to blow them up. They also do a better job of insulating you from the cold ground than most air mattresses do. But if you can sleep on one, you are a hardier person than I am. They don't provide much cushion.

**INFLATABLE MATTRESS**

This takes up more space than a foam mattress but it also provides more cushion—adjustable cushion. A huge drawback is that these beds tend to deflate and get holes in them for no apparent reason. More than one person has woken up in the middle of the night with a completely deflated air mattress. Energetic sex is guaranteed to take the air out of your mattress. Best advice is to pack a spare.

**COT**

The newest models look and fold up like lawn chairs, but most are space hogs. The folding military style is a bit more compact and better built. Look for cots that do not have a bar running horizontally across the middle as bars kill your back. Make sure your cot has a mattress of its own, or put a foam mattress on it.

# A Good Night's Sleep

No matter which bed you choose, layer your bedding to provide breathable warmth and insulation. If you're sleeping on a cot or air mattress, you are sleeping suspended in the air, and that results in loss of body heat, even if you are snuggled up with someone smokin' hot. If the temperature at night is lower than the daytime temperature, condensation may soak through the top layer of your bedding. If the night is warmer than you expected, layers allow you to peel off blankets until you're cool enough to sleep.

- The first layer is a wool blanket that goes directly on your cot or mattress. If the nights are cold, double this layer. Spritz this layer with lavender spray for some aromatherapy while you sleep.

- For the second and third layer, use a fitted and then a flat sheet set. If you are sensitive to wool, use sheets with a higher thread count. The cooler the weather, the fuzzier the sheets you should pack.

- The fourth layer is a comforter or thick blanket. If you are camping where it gets quite cool at night, opt for a down comforter. This is the layer you remove if you don't need as many blankets.

- The fifth (and top) layer is a wool blanket. Wool keeps you warm even when it's damp; it breathes nicely, dries quickly, and protects your other bedding from condensation.

Each morning, as long as it isn't raining out, hang your bedding out to dry. It should only take an hour or so to dry, and you'll be much happier if you do this. Not only will your bedding be dry, but your tent won't smell like a locker room.

# CAMPING Olympics

Bring back the old-fashioned fun and games! Having scheduled activities for your family or group combined with plenty of time for relaxation is a solid recipe for a great camping trip. With adults you can be as competitive as you want, with children you may want to tone that down or focus on cooperative games instead. Add in games or puzzles that exercise your mind, too. You can host the games over a series of days and reward the winners on the last day. Who wouldn't want a medal for Best Egg Roller or Most Helpful Player?

Get physical and silly with a series of races: three-legged races, egg rolling, or horseback. Remember to keep it fun and use common sense safety precautions. With races like these, it's more about the thrill of laughter than the agony of skinned knees. The exercise isn't a bad thing, either.

Would you rather use your brains and cooperate, rather than compete? Try Iron Age: Council of the Clans, a historical strategy game.

IRON AGE
COUNCIL OF THE CLAN

A Table-top Strategy Game
of Power, Honour, and Democracy

by Brendan Myers

"Iron Age" is a tabletop political strategy and debating game, in which players compete and co-operate with each other to build a community. The better you manage your village, and the better you manage your relations with other players, the more honor you will gain. And the more honor you gain, the better your position will be at a special democratic assembly called the Landsmoot, where one player will be elected the Chieftain. If you can get yourself elected Chieftain often enough, and remain the chieftain long enough, you win! This game is so fun, your kids won't notice the historical or political lessons they're learning. It is helpful if you bring a small white board or larger tablet of paper when you play the game.

Looking for a new game to play while camping? Try Kubb, better known as Viking Chess. I was introduced to this yard game by my friend Heather Biedermann while on a a recent camping trip and it was a blast! Viking Chess is much different than the board game. Yes, there's strategy, but you're throwing sticks and trying to knock stuff over, which makes sense in a Viking game. The game is played over a modest expanse of grass and the object is to knock over the kubbs on the opposing side, then knock the "king" over, before the opponent does. It's a bit more complicated than that, which is what  you'd expect from a game with chess in its name, but still fun for kids age 7 or older as long as they are playing with adults.

What ever games you decide to play, keep in the mind you win by having fun and enjoying time spent with one another without the usual outside distractions.

# FEEL GOOD ABOUT LIGHT

The LuminAID is a solar-powered, inflatable, and water-resistant light that packs flat and provides up to 15 hours of light. It's small enough that you can stick it in your back pocket. If you buy one through the company's Get Light, Give Light program, LuminAID will give a second light to someone in a disaster situation or someone in a developing country who doesn't have access to nontoxic lighting.

# CHOOSE THE BEST CHAIR

I've had camp chairs break on me. It's painful and embarrassing. I've had chairs designed so poorly if you leaned back in them, they tipped over backward. I found this out while holding a knife and a potato. I've also owned chairs so uncomfortable no one would sit in them. It's taken me years and wasted money to find decent chairs for camping. Here are a few tips to help you find the best chair.

## WEIGHT

I won't dance around this: when you're looking for camp chairs, your weight and size matter most. If you're a heavier or larger person, try director-style camping chairs. They don't fold up quite as small, but they're wider and rated for three hundred pounds and heavier. Even if you're tiny, these are more comfortable than your average camp chair.

## SIT UP OR LEAN BACK

Do you like to sit up straighter or slump and slouch? If you prefer to slouch, look for a chair with more give to it. A butterfly chair is ideal. Make sure you get a sturdy metal chair and not a cheap dorm-style butterfly chair. If you like to sit up straighter, consider a folding chair. They aren't nearly as compact as traditional camp chairs, but they give more support and are better for when you eat at a table.

## EXTREMES

There are also floor pillows, stools, and loungers. Loungers are for lounging, and there isn't too much that can beat them. They provide support all along your body and neck, but are horrid for trying to eat in. As for small stools? Very compact and handy, but are uncomfortable to sit on for more than an hour. Floor pillows are a great option for additional seating, especially if they're on a rug. You do have a rug, right?

# ONE *chair* THREE *ways*

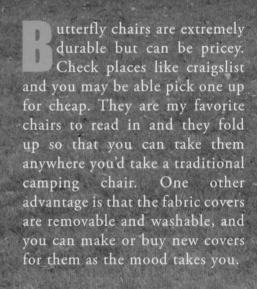

**B**utterfly chairs are extremely durable but can be pricey. Check places like craigslist and you may be able pick one up for cheap. They are my favorite chairs to read in and they fold up so that you can take them anywhere you'd take a traditional camping chair. One other advantage is that the fabric covers are removable and washable, and you can make or buy new covers for them as the mood takes you.

This tan chair takes on a very feminine look with a fuzzy pink blanket and floral throw pillow. Pink accents follow through with a traditional cosmo in a mason jar and a plate of petit fours. The dainty side table could be more flirty with a faded coat of white paint.

The high contrast of black and white gives a more tailored look while the floral print on the pillow saves it from being to stark. The rug is a made of polypropylene so it can weather rain or shine. A dirty martini and chocolate truffles pamper with class.

A bright blue chair cover gives a more modern and masculine edge to the classic safari look. The solid wood traveling bar and pewter dishes bring an exotic African Queen type flair while the fern print pillow and natural fiber rug firmly ground the look.

# KEEP IT CLEAN:
## *shower*

A hot-water shower in the great outdoors anytime you want it isn't a pipe dream. There are now affordable portable hot-water-on-demand showers that run off propane. Just hang the unit up on a handy tree, hook it to a garden hose, and add a privacy screen. Much better than waiting in line at a communal bathroom.

# KEEP IT EASY:
## starting a fire

**A** crackling campfire is the star of the show while camping, but isn't always easy to get going. If your firestarting skills are a bit rusty, try using a tea light. Place a small log in the center of your pit. Place the tea light next to the log and lean thin twigs against the log and across the candle. Place a few larger sticks on top of the twigs. Now light the candle. With a continuous flame on the sticks for two hours, your fire will light! Once the sticks catch fire, add larger sticks and logs until you have a solid fire going, and please follow all fire safety rules.

# Comfort Drinks
## AND
# Recipes

EGG SANDWICH

# Egg Sandwich

The lowly egg sandwich gets a face-lift with maple bacon, spicy mayo, and pickled spring onions. Make the mayo ahead of time.

## INGREDIENTS

4 spring onions, thinly sliced
½ cup apple cider vinegar
2 teaspoons sugar
1 teaspoon salt
12 slices of maple-cured bacon
1/4 cup mayo with 1 tablespoon sriracha added
¼ cup mayo, plain
2 tablespoons butter
4 eggs
8 slices good bread

## DIRECTIONS

In a small bowl, combine the first 4 ingredients. Let set for 30 minutes.
Cook bacon in a skillet and drain cooked pieces on a paper towel.
While bacon is cooking and onions are pickling, spread 1 side of bread with plain mayo and fry over medium-low heat until browned (about 3 minutes).
When done with bread, add butter to skillet and fry eggs to desired doneness. Salt and pepper the eggs to taste.
Spread the untoasted side of the bread with some of the spicy mayo, then layer the bacon, egg, and onion.

# Hot Chocolate

I'm a hot chocolate fiend, which is weird because I'm not a big fan of sweets. Here are two different versions of hot chocolate for you to try while gazing into the dancing flames of your fire.

## WHITE CHOCOLATE & LAVENDER
### INGREDIENTS

1 cup of milk, hot
1 heaping tablespoon of mini white-chocolate chips
1 tablespoon lavender flowers

### DIRECTIONS

Put the lavender flowers in a tea strainer and let steep in the hot milk for 3 minutes. Remove the strainer and add the chocolate chips; stir until dissolved.

## DARK CHOCOLATE & SPICES
### INGREDIENTS

1 cup of milk
1 heaping tablespoon of mini dark chocolate chips
1 pinch each cinnamon, chipotle powder, cayenne, and nutmeg

### DIRECTIONS

Add the spices to the milk and gently simmer for 5 minutes, taking care not to let come to a boil. Pour into a mug with the chocolate chips, stir to dissolve, and enjoy.

# Roasted Veggie Mac 'n' Cheese

Mac 'n' cheese tops many peoples' comfort-food lists. Adding roasted veggies to it, with their smoky sweet flavor, fits perfectly with summer alfresco dining. I've included alternative ingredients to make the recipe gluten-free (GF).

## INGREDIENTS

3 cups each broccoli florets, sliced tomatoes, and sliced onion
2 tablespoons olive oil
3 tablespoons butter or butter substitute
3 tablespoons flour or gluten-free flour
4 cups warm milk
2 cups shredded asiago cheese
2 ¾ cups shredded cheddar cheese
1 pound penne or spiral pasta, cooked and drained (GF)
Salt and pepper to taste

## DIRECTIONS

Slice the tomatoes 1/4 inch thick and the onions 1/8 inch thick. Toss the veggies with the oil and roast over campfire. Whisk the butter and flour in a medium-size pot over medium-high heat until mixed, then add milk and simmer until thickened. Remove from heat after 5 minutes. Whisk in the cheese, salt, and pepper until smooth. Add in pasta and veggies and fold in carefully. Heat on low for an additional 10 minutes, then serve.

# Meat Loaf Patties with Gravy

Frying the meat loaf patties in a pan turns this comfort-food favorite into a camping favorite. Just make the patties at home and freeze them. The Roquefort gravy is to die for! Pour it over the meat loaf patties and mashed potatoes.

## MEATLOAF PATTIES

### INGREDIENTS

1 ½ pounds ground beef
1 egg
1 onion, chopped
1 cup milk

1 cup dried bread crumbs
(can substitute GF bread crumbs)
Salt and pepper to taste

### DIRECTIONS

Mix everything together in a large bowl. Form into 8 patties and freeze or use. Cook them by frying in a pan like any other hamburger.

## ROQUEFORT GRAVY

### INGREDIENTS

1 cup heavy cream
½ cup beef broth

6 ounces Roquefort crumbles
Salt to taste; go light

### DIRECTIONS

Combine all ingredients in a small pan and simmer, very gently. This gravy takes 2 hours or so, but is worth it. It can be made at home ahead of time and brought in your cooler, but I've made it while camping. It gives you a great excuse to relax for an afternoon with a glass of wine: "I'm watching the gravy, sorry, can't move!"

# Bananas Star Foster

Bananas are a great fruit to take on a camping trip as they are more durable than you think and can just be set out or hung up—no special storage needed. This gooey treat can be served over ice cream or French toast, but is most fun at night, when everyone can see it flambé. I add small, edible gold stars which are found in the cake decorating aisle of craft store, just before serving.

## INGREDIENTS

¼ cup butter
2/3 cup brown sugar
4 tablespoons rum, 151 proof or higher
1 ½ teaspoons vanilla
½ teaspoon cinnamon
3 bananas, cut into 1-inch-thick slices

## DIRECTIONS

In a skillet over medium heat, combine butter, sugar, vanilla, and cinnamon.
When mixture begins to bubble, add in bananas and cook for 1 minute.
Add in rum and, using a match or lighter, carefully light the rum on fire. When the flames burn out, the bananas are done.

# Resources

*"Where did you get that?"*

When I see camping gear I like I'm not shy  about asking that question. I'll ask them what they like best about it, what they don't like about it, and if they'd buy it again. All of the gear pictured in this book are items that I would, and sometimes have, purchased again.

Some gear I can't find anywhere except in my brain so I make it myself or work with a craftsperson to create it. One such piece is the portable wood bar seen in chapter three's Essential Products. This is the very first piece of furniture in the Martinis & Marshmallows camping and outdoor living line. New pieces are being designed and added to my store, which can be found at https://www.etsy.com/shop/MnMGlamping

Other places I frequently shop are Sportsmansguide.com, IKEA, craigslist.org, department stores, and traditional camping outfitters and stores. Chances are if you saw a product in this book you liked, it came from one of those places. If you'd like to ask me about a product in more detail, you can find me here:

Facebook:  facebook.com/MartinisandMarshmallows

Twitter:  @Cara_Schulz

My blog:  http://martinisandmarshmallows.com/

# Acknowledgements

No book is the sole creation of the author. It is brought into existence through the efforts of many people, some of whom may not know the impact they have had on an author's life and work.

In 2004 I had the great fortune to be hired by EXHIBITOR magazine and work with its president, Randal Acker and the Founder of the company, Lee Knight. Not only is Randy a wonderful human being and Lee a true visionary, they opened up a new world to me: event and exhibit design. Many of the ideas in this book were inspired by the years I spent immersed in the industry and the creative people I met. Bendickson, I'm looking at you.

Randy encouraged me to join the International Special Events Society, a creative and talented group of people. Many of them are dear and lasting friends and this book wouldn't have happened without them. Thank you members of ISES-Minneapolis/St. Paul. Words can't express how much I learned from you.

Thanks also to those who went above and beyond the call of friendship to assist with this book: my friends Jim, Kenny, Heather, and Andy, and my sister Teri for allowing me to use your backyards for shoots; Jim and Kenny (again), and my family, Lonny, Selene, Emily, Sarah, Nicole, Evan, and Connor for being my models; thanks to my childhood friend Kathi Finley, for allowing me to borrow her gandson Mason for a few photographs; special thanks to Mallory who agreed to do the shower shoot in 40 degree weather in November; my partners in crime and cheerleaders Crystal Blanton, Teo Bishop, Peter Dybing, Star Foster, Devin Hunter, Laura LaVoie, Yeshe Rabbit, David Salisbury, Jason Pitz-Waters, and Heather Biedermann. We've been on so many crazy adventures together. There's so many more yet to have.

Last, but not at all least, I'd like to thank those who backed my Kickstarter. If these people hadn't taken a chance on me, you wouldn't be holding this book:

Matt Belitsos

Mary Bergman

Heather Biedermann

Lisa Marie Borchert

Kenny Christopher

T Thorn Coyle

Steffanie Crossland

Laura LaVoie

Jim Leighton

Lāhela Nihipali

Yeshe Rabbit

Nick Ritter

David Salisbury

Nate & Gail Snyder

Joe Szurszewski

I owe you all a drink.

# Team Bios

Author Cara Schulz is a journalist and author who lives in Minneapolis with her husband and cat. She loves glamping, red wine, and doesn't have any tattoos.

Editor Kathryn Hinds is a teacher, editor, poet, novelist, short-story writer, and author of more than fifty nonfiction books for young adults. Visit her online at www.kathrynhinds.com. Photo by Fox Gradin, Celestial Studios Photography.

Interior book designer Ericka Darst is a graphic artist located in Minneapolis, specializing in publication layout, stationery, and branding design. You can find her work at www.edarstdesign.com and contact her at eadarst@yahoo.com

Cover artist Kit Foster is a multi-award winning graphic designer who specializes in book cover design. He lives with his fiancée and daughter just outside Edinburgh, Scotland, the world's first City of Literature. You can contact Kit at kitfosterdesign@gmail.com